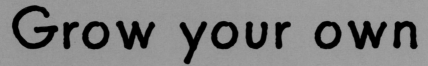

Grow your own

Potatoes

Helen Lanz

W

FRANKLIN WATTS

LONDON•SYDNEY

To Mark because your head reminds me of a potato

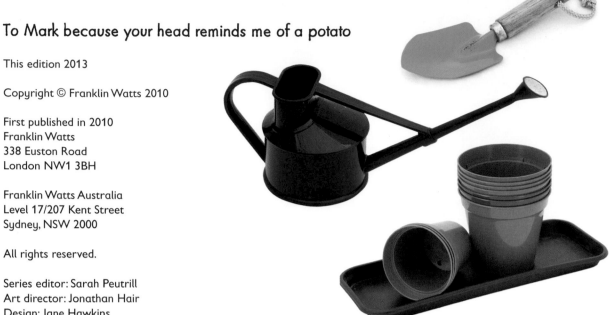

This edition 2013

Copyright © Franklin Watts 2010

First published in 2010
Franklin Watts
338 Euston Road
London NW1 3BH

Franklin Watts Australia
Level 17/207 Kent Street
Sydney, NSW 2000

Series editor: Sarah Peutrill
Art director: Jonathan Hair
Design: Jane Hawkins
Photography: Victoria Coombs/Ecoscene (unless otherwise credited)

Credits: Tomas Bercic/istockphoto: 12b. Courtesy of Crown © FERA /SPL: 20b. Richard Goerg/istockphoto: 9bl. Joe Gough/istockphoto: 6c. GFDL/CC 2.5: 20m. Marjanneke de Jong/Shutterstock: 25b. Kativ/istockphoto: 21br. Helen Lanz: 10t, 19t, 23. Monkey Business/Shutterstock: 26t. Moodboard/Corbis: front cover b. Dan Moore/istockphoto: 1, 31. Penny Oakley: 7m, 15t, 15b, 16m and 18b. Vibeke Olsen/istockphoto: 20t. Quanthem/istockphoto: 6b. Dr Marlin E Rice/AgstockUSA/SPL: 21tr. Steve Snyder/istockphoto: 21bl. Liz Van Steenburgh/Shutterstock: 27b. Sally Wallis/Shutterstock: front cover t.
Every attempt has been made to clear copyright. Should there be any inadvertent omission please apply to the publisher for rectification.

Thanks to Jasmine Clarke and Tony Field, seasoned gardeners, for kindly sharing their gardening knowledge.

The author and publisher would like to thank the models who took part in this book.

Dewey number: 635.2'1
ISBN: 978 1 4451 1786 7
Printed in China

Franklin Watts is a division of Hachette Children's Books, an Hachette UK company.
www.hachette.co.uk

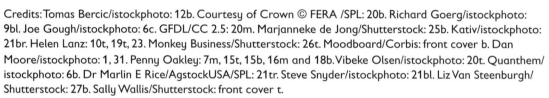

Safety notice:

Gardening is fun! There are a few basic rules you should always follow, however. Always garden with an adult; any pesticides and fertilisers should be handled by adults only and applied to specified plants only; wear appropriate clothing and footwear and always wash your hands when you have finished in the garden.

Contents

Words in **bold** are in the glossary on page 29.

Why grow your own potatoes?

Do you like to eat sausage and mashed potato or how about chips? Most of us like to *eat* potatoes in one form or another. But have you ever thought about *growing* them?

▲ Potatoes can be cooked in all sorts of ways: mashed, baked, fried, boiled, chipped or roasted. What's your favourite way?

Fresh flavour

You will never cut through a fresher, crispier potato than one you've just pulled up from your garden. Often, fruit and vegetables that you have grown yourself have real flavour, partly because you can eat them straight after they have been picked.

◄ Potatoes that you cook straight from the garden are hard, crisp and dense.

Room to grow

You don't need much room to grow your own potatoes either. Did you know that you can grow them in a bag or pot if you don't have a vegetable plot?

But one of the best things about growing your own potatoes is that it's fun!

▲ You can grow potatoes in small places – even in buckets and bags!

Flower

Leaf

Stem

Root

Young tuber

Old seed potato

SCIENCE SPOT *What is a tuber?*

The potato is a stem tuber. A tuber is a **bulbous** growth that grows on the stem or root of a plant. The bulbous stem tuber stores food, or **nutrients**, for the plant but it can also be dug up and eaten – this is the actual potato.

Be prepared!

So, you've decided to grow your own! It's a good idea to think about what you will need before you get going.

Think ahead

You will be outside a lot digging around in dirt so you will need some old clothes that your parents or carers won't mind if you get dirty. And for your feet, some wellies or old trainers will do the job.

You also need to decide where you will be planting your potatoes – in a pot, bag or in the ground.

▶ If you are planting in a pot or bag, you will need some soil. ▼

What else do I need?

You may decide to use gardening gloves, but these aren't necessary. A fork and trowel may be useful.

You will definitely need some **seed potatoes** (you can buy a bag of these from a garden centre). A cardboard egg box is useful right at the start to **chit** your potatoes (see pages 12–13).

Finally, you will need a watering can and some plant food to help your potatoes to grow.

PLANT FOOD

500ml ℮

Top tip!

It's a good idea to keep a growing diary, writing down everything, from the potato type to how and when you did things. This will help if you decide to do it again, and will be fun to look back on. If you have a camera, taking photos as you go along would also be a good idea.

Choose your variety

There are a lot of potato **varieties** to choose from.

▲ Rocket potatoes are good for boiling.

Estima   Kestrel

▲ Estima is a popular variety to grow: it is good for mashing, boiling and baking. Kestrel potatoes are good for chipping and roasting.

First earlies

First earlies can be planted early in the growing season (see page 28), but after the main **frosts**, and should be ready to **harvest** about 10 weeks later. Many first early potatoes avoid a lot of the problems that sometimes affect potatoes, such as **blight** (see page 20). Varieties of early potato include Rocket, Maris Bard and Duke of York.

Second earlies and salad potatoes

Plant second earlies and salad varieties at the beginning of the growing season, but just after first earlies. These will usually take about 13 weeks before they are ready to harvest. Second early varieties include: Estima, Kestrel and Maris Peer. Salad, or new, potatoes include the Charlotte variety.

Main crop

These can be planted in the middle of the growing season. They take about 20 weeks before they are ready to harvest. Main crop varieties can get more **diseases** and **pests** (see Top tip below and pages 20–21) so it is worth checking which varieties best survive such problems. Maris Piper, King Edward and Melody are main crop potatoes.

► These are Desiree potatoes, a main crop variety.

Maris Piper

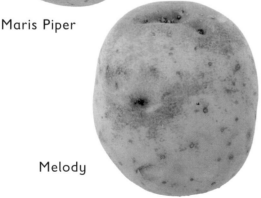

Melody

▲ Maris Piper is a good, all-round cooking variety. Melody potatoes don't often get diseases.

Top tip!

Check the seed potato bag to see exactly when you should plant your chosen variety, what diseases that particular variety generally avoids and how best to cook it. You can also check the Internet or ask at your local garden centre.

Chit the tuber

eye

Potatoes grow from seed potatoes, rather than seeds. These are older potatoes that have been stored, and start to **sprout** 'eyes'. You need to encourage your seed potatoes to sprout a bit more before planting. This is called chitting.

▲ *The eyes are the buds that grow into the new potato plants.*

Free from disease

It is a good idea to buy seed potatoes from a garden centre, rather than just use old potatoes from your cupboard that have started to chit. These may carry a disease that the original potato had. This will be passed on to any potatoes that grow from the old potato.

▶ *Properly grown seed potatoes are unlikely to carry diseases.*

Step by step

1. Before the start of the growing season (see page 28), prepare your seed potatoes. Check the bag to see when you should plant your variety of potato. Chit them about four or so weeks before planting.

2. To start your seed potatoes, choose a number of healthy-looking chitting potatoes.

3. Place each seed potato in the bottom of an egg carton, one potato in each cell, with the eyes upwards.

4. Put the egg carton on a bright windowsill, but not in direct sunlight. Leave to sprout for four or so weeks.

Top tip!

As your potatoes sprout, the sprouts should be green, not white. If they are white, they are not getting enough light so move them to a new spot.

Pot or plot?

▲ Potatoes prefer slightly acidic soil, but will grow in any soil (see pages 24–25).

To help keep your trench straight, you can use string tied to two bits of wood at either end of your trench. ▼

While your seed potatoes are chitting, you can prepare your pot or plot.

The best place

Potatoes love warm and sunny spots, with plenty of direct sunlight and no shady bits — they don't like the frost at all. They also like **well-drained soil**.

Preparing the plot

If you are going to grow your potatoes in the ground, you will need to prepare the soil well — digging in plenty of **compost**. Do this in good time and keep working the soil over.

Dig your **trench** about 12cm deep. If you have more than one row, make sure the rows are about 60cm apart.

Top tip!

Potatoes do need a good depth (height) of soil to grow in, but early varieties don't need too much room.

Preparing the pot (or bag!)

Early potatoes will also grow well in a large pot, bin or even a bin bag. You will need to make sure there are holes in the bottom to allow the water to drain out.

Then put gravel and large stones into the bottom of your bin or bag to help with **drainage**.

Put in a mixture of soil and compost until it is at least 12cm deep.

Top tip!

The bin or bag will get very heavy when you put the soil in, so position it where you want it before you fill it with soil.

Sowing the seed potato

When the sprouts on the seed potatoes are about 1.5cm long (four or so weeks after chitting) your seed potatoes are ready to plant outside.

Step-by-step

1. Make sure you place the seed potato in the soil with the shoots pointing up.

2. In the vegetable plot, plant your seed potatoes about 30cm apart from each other.

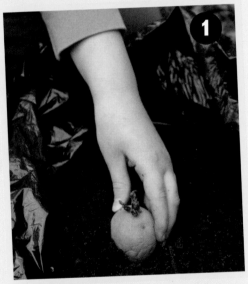

SCIENCE SPOT

What it takes to grow

Most plants start out as seeds (or in a potato's case, a seed potato). To grow, or **germinate**, seeds need dark, damp and warm conditions – soil is the perfect place. The roots develop first; these take up water and nutrients from the soil, which are then moved all round the plant through its veins.

3. For potatoes in pots, you will need about 15cm of space between each potato and some space between the potato and the side of the bag or bin. Place the first seed potato in the middle of the bag and arrange the others around it.

4. Cover the potatoes with about 7.5cm of soil. Be careful not to damage the shoots. For those in the vegetable plot, use the soil that has come out of the trench to cover your seed potatoes.

Top tip!

If you use a large plant pot, rather than a bin, just have two or three seed potatoes in it.

Tending the crop

As soon as you have planted your seed potatoes, water them well.

Water well

Check your potatoes regularly to see if they need a drink, especially in hot weather. However, make sure the soil does not become **waterlogged**. To see if you need to water, poke your finger into the soil. If it is damp, you may not need to water just yet.

▲ Some watering cans have special spray heads – but you don't have to use one of these.

◄ Soil may look dry on the top, but be damp underneath.

Earthing up

Two weeks after the first green shoots appear, you will need to cover the plants up again! This is called 'earthing up'. Because potatoes are stem tubers, they grow on the stem of the plant. As the plant grows taller, the potatoes therefore emerge above the soil. However, too much light turns the tuber green. To stop them going green, cover the plant with soil every two to three weeks.

◀ It is not safe to eat green potatoes – they will give you tummy ache.

▲ The first green shoots will begin to appear after about two weeks.

Green potatoes

◀ It seems odd to cover the plants with soil, but be sure to leave the tops of the plants showing through. Throw away any green potatoes.

Give them a feed!

Ask your grown-up helper to add liquid feed to your plants in containers about a month after planting them.

PLANT FOOD

500ml

Pest patrol!

Checking your potatoes regularly is the best way to keep them healthy. If you do spot any problems, you can deal with them quickly.

Blight

This is the one of the worst diseases that potatoes can get. It affects the leaves first and eventually can affect the whole plant, including the growing potatoes themselves.

◄ *If you notice brown patches like this, your plant has blight. It is best to remove the infected plant and throw it away.*

Common scab

This disease affects just the skin of the potato. It can help to dig in lots of compost or **manure** before you plant your seed potatoes as potatoes in dry or light soil seem to get it the most.

▼ *This potato has scab – raised patches that can split the surface.*

Top tip!
Both blight and common scab affect potatoes later in the growing season, so why not choose an early variety to grow to start with and hopefully you won't have these problems to deal with.

Slugs and wireworms

Wireworms are the grubs of the click beetle. They tunnel into the growing potatoes and ruin them. Digging the earth well before planting helps protect against wireworm. Remove any that you find as you dig.

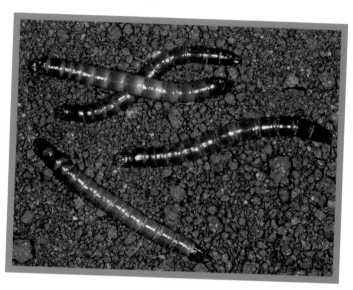

▲ Wireworms make holes in potatoes.

▲ A pond or shallow container of water may attract frogs, the gardener's best friend!

Sorting out slugs

If you do have trouble with slugs, you could try to combat them by encouraging hedgehogs, frogs and so on into garden to eat them! Or you can pick slugs off your crops.

▲ Hungry slugs like to snack on potatoes.

Harvest

Having looked after your crop well, it won't be long before it's time for harvest.

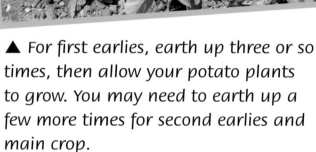

▲ For first earlies, earth up three or so times, then allow your potato plants to grow. You may need to earth up a few more times for second earlies and main crop.

How long?

If you have planted a first early variety, your potato crop should be ready 10 or so weeks after planting. If you have planted a second early variety or main crop potato, these will take a little longer to grow (see page 28). You can tell when your crop is ready as the plants will often flower. When the plant flowers, check for potatoes.

If you find some and they are the size of hen's eggs they're ready, so dig deep! It's like looking for buried treasure!

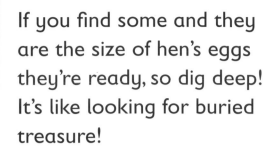

Enjoy your find!

Top tip!

Only take the amount of potatoes you need; leave the others in the ground to continue growing. If you do store picked potatoes, keep them in cloth or paper sacks in a dark, dry place.

23

What sort of soil?

Potatoes grow happily in different types of soil. They do prefer slightly acidic soil, but will grow in any.

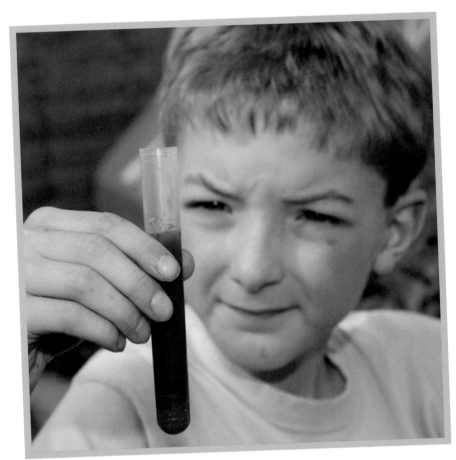

How acidic?

Soil can be neutral (pH of 7), acid (pH below 7) or alkaline (pH above 7). You can test your soil to see what pH it is. You can buy a kit from your local garden centre.

◀ *Soil-testing kits are quick and easy to use.*

Different types of soil

There are also different types of soil. The main types are sandy, silty or clay. Soil may vary in different places even around your garden.

◀ *This soil is mostly clay.*

Do a hand test to see what yours is:

sandy – feels gritty to touch; won't hold together as a ball; warms up quickly, so helps plants' growth, but dries out quickly

silty – feels smooth; will roll but not hold together as a ball; is best soil type for growing most plants

clay – feels sticky; can roll it into a ball; retains moisture well

It is possible to have a combination of these.

▶ *Sandy soil will run through your fingers easily.*

Top tip!

When you know your soil type, you can choose potato plants that best suit your soil. Check online, on the seed packet, or ask at your local garden centre. You can also add things, such as fertilisers and compost, to your soil to change its pH.

▼ *Digging in compost makes your soil less alkaline and better for growing potatoes.*

Perfect potatoes

Potatoes are a tasty food that can be enjoyed in many ways. They are good for you too! Potatoes are very **nutritious**. They contain **vitamins** B, B6 and C, as well as the important **mineral**, potassium.

Preparing your potatoes

Before you get creative with you potatoes, you need to give them a good wash in cold water. You may need a potato scrubber for stubborn dirt.

▲ *Don't forget to eat the skin as many of the vitamins are stored here.*

Potato recipes

Potatoes cannot be eaten raw, but there are many ways to cook them. You can boil, bake, roast or fry them. Baking in their jackets is one of the healthiest ways as there's lots of **fibre** in the skin. Many recipes include potatoes, from cottage pie to soups and stews. Why not try the recipe opposite, or search the Internet for more ideas?

Make a potato crusted pizza

Ingredients
- 400g large British maincrop potatoes, peeled
- 175g self-raising flour
- 1 teaspoon (tsp) baking powder
- 2 tsp mixed dried herbs
- 150 ml milk

Topping:
- 150g broccoli florets
- 2 tablespoons (tbsp) tomato puree
- 2 tomatoes, 1 pepper,
- 50g cheese, grated

With your grown-up helper:

1. Cut the potatoes into small pieces and boil in water for 10 minutes. Steam the broccoli for a few minutes then put to one side. Drain the potatoes well and allow to cool, then mash.

2. Sift the flour and baking powder into a bowl. Stir in the potato and herbs. Add the milk and mix to form a soft dough. Tip this out onto a floured surface and knead lightly to form a smooth ball.

4. Place the ball onto a greased baking sheet. Press it out evenly into a 23cm circle. Put into the oven at 225°C/Gas 7 and bake for 10 minutes.

5. Remove the base and lower the oven temperature to 200°C/Gas 6.

6. Spread the tomato puree over the base; slice the tomato and pepper and arrange on top, then scatter over the broccoli and cheese.

7. Bake in the oven for a further 8–10 minutes until the cheese has melted and the edge of the base is crisp.

Growing calendar

Here's an 'at-a-glance' guide to the growing year. Planting and growing times vary, depending on where you live.

Early winter (Dec–Jan)

Plan your crop. Choose your potato varieties.

Late winter (Jan–Feb)

Dig over your plot, adding compost or manure.

Chit first early seed potatoes for four weeks at the end of this period.

Early spring (March–April)

Plant first early varieties at the beginning of this period.

Chit second early seed potatoes for four weeks at the beginning of this period. Chit main crop potatoes for four weeks in the middle of this period.

Water, feed and earth up first earlies. Cover potatoes if frosty.

Late spring (April–May)

Plant second early varieties at the beginning of this period. Plant main crop potatoes in the middle of this period.

Keep checking, watering, earthing up and feeding your first and second earlies and main crop potatoes.

Early summer (June–July)

Keep checking, watering, earthing up and feeding your second earlies.

First earlies will be ready for harvest.

Late summer (July–Aug)

Keep checking, watering, earthing up and feeding your main crop potatoes.

Second earlies will be ready for harvest.

Early autumn (Sept–Oct)

Main crop potatoes will be ready for harvest.

Late autumn (Oct–Nov)

Dig over your plot, adding compost or manure ready for next year's crop.

Gardening glossary

blight: a disease that is especially bad for potatoes.

bulbous: something that is a big, bulging shape.

chit: to encourage seed potatoes to sprout before planting.

compost: a mixture of soil and rotting plants used to fertilise, or feed, plants to help them grow.

disease: an illness.

drainage: in this case, to allow water to flow through the soil and leave the plant pot or bag, so the plant's roots don't rot.

fibre: the roughage in food, such as the skin of fruit or a potato.

frost: frozen water droplets that freeze on the ground on cold mornings.

germinate: the point when a root and leaf break through a seed case and the seed begins to grow.

harvest: the gathering in of crops, in this case, vegetables.

manure: fertiliser, waste from animals such as horses and pigs.

minerals: natural substances that are in food that are good for your body and health.

nutrients: something that gives goodness needed for growing or being healthy.

nutritious: something that is healthy for you to eat.

pests: insects or animals that are destructive to a plant, such as slugs or greenfly.

root: the part of a plant below the ground that takes the nutrients, or goodness, from the soil to the rest of the plant.

seed potatoes: the tuber that is used to grow new potato plants.

sprout: to produce new growth such as the 'eyes' of a potato.

trench: a small ditch in the soil to plant the seed potatoes in.

varieties: types of a plant.

vitamins: natural substances that are in food that are good for your body and health.

waterlogged: over-watered, or wet.

well-drained soil: soil that allows water to seep out of it, so that the soil doesn't get too wet and soggy.

Index

Useful websites

www.bbc.co.uk/gardening/gardening_with_children/

www.gardeningwithchildren.co.uk
Gardening activities and information about how plants grow.

www.rhs.org.uk/schoolgardening
Find out about school gardening projects and clubs or play the gardening game.

www.britishpotatoes.co.uk/the-potato
Find out all you need to know, and more, about potatoes!

Gardening club

Have you enjoyed growing your own? How about joining a gardening club? Your school may have one. You could grow fruit and vegetables which could be cooked and eaten as part of your school meals and snacks, or make ladybird homes to help attract them to your garden. If your school doesn't have a gardening club, why not talk to your teacher about setting one up?